AMERICA
in the
FIFTIES

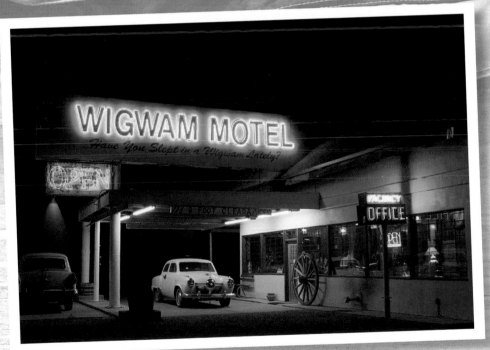

ENZO GEORGE

Cavendish Square

New York

Published in 2016 by Cavendish Square Publishing, LLC
243 5th Avenue, Suite 136, New York, NY 10016

© 2016 Brown Bear Books Ltd

First Edition

Website: cavendishsq.com

This publication represents the opinions and views of the author based on his or her personal experiences, knowledge, and research. The information in this book serves as a general guide only. the author and publisher have used their best efforts in preparing this book and disclaim liability rising directly or indirectly from the use and application of this book.

CPSIA Compliance Information: Batch #WS15CSQ

All websites were available and accurate when this book was sent to press.

Library of Congress Cataloging-in-Publication Data

George, Enzo.
America in the fifties / Enzo George.
     pages cm. — (Primary sources in U.S. history)
Includes bibliographical references and index.
ISBN 978-1-50260-494-1 (hardcover) — ISBN 978-1-50260-495-8 (ebook)
1. United States—Civilization—1945--Juvenile literature. 2. United States—Social life and customs—1945-1970—
Juvenile literature. 3. Nineteen fifties—Juvenile literature. I. Title.

E169.12.G47 2015
973.918—dc23

2014049223

For Brown Bear Books Ltd:
Editorial Director: Lindsey Lowe
Managing Editor: Tim Cooke
Children's Publisher: Anne O'Daly
Design Manager: Keith Davis
Designer: Lynne Lennon
Picture Manager: Sophie Mortimer

Manufactured in the United States of America

CONTENTS

INTRODUCTION

Primary sources are the best way to get close to people from the past. They include the things people wrote in diaries, letters, or books; the paintings, drawings, maps, or cartoons they created; and even the buildings they constructed, the clothes they wore, or the possessions they owned. Such sources often reveal a lot about how people saw themselves and how they thought about their world.

This book collects a range of primary sources from the late 1940s and the 1950s. The atmosphere of the period was a combination of optimism based on economic prosperity and tension caused by the threat of war from the Communist Soviet Union.

The nature of the 1950s was formed in the late 1940s, when millions of veterans returned from World War II (1939–1945). They started families and moved to new suburbs. People explored the country using the new road network. Teenagers became an identifiable group, with their own fashions, music, and interests. Meanwhile, fear of Communism led to U.S. involvement in the Korean War (1950–1953) and other international affairs. The tension with the Soviet Union known as the Cold War is the subject of another book in this series, as is the African-American struggle for civil rights.

HOW TO USE THIS BOOK

Each spread contains at least one primary source. Look out for "Source Explored" boxes that explain images from the 1950s and who made them and why. There are also "As They Saw It" boxes that contain quotes from people of the period.

Some boxes contain more detailed information about a particular aspect of a subject. The subjects are arranged in roughly chronological order. They focus on key events or people. There is a full timeline of the period at the back of the book.

Some spreads feature a longer extract from a contemporary eyewitness. Look for the colored introduction that explains who the writer is and the origin of his or her account. These accounts are often accompanied by a related visual primary source.

THE POSTWAR WORLD

At the end of World War II in 1945, millions of returning veterans needed jobs. Many women who had left their homes to work in factories and on farms during the war were replaced and became unemployed. An economic downturn marked the end of the decade. President Harry S. Truman was determined to steer the country back to prosperity.

▼ Stacks of supplies on the way to Europe from U.S. warehouses as part of the Marshall Plan.

▼ This poster encouraged veterans to enter higher education under the terms of the G.I. Bill of Rights.

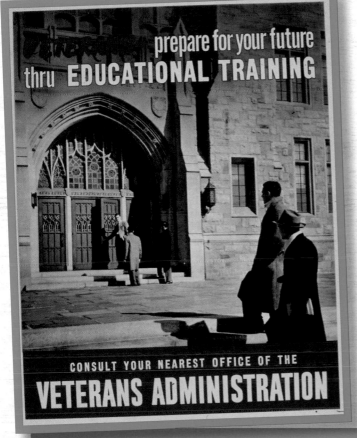

prepare for your future thru **EDUCATIONAL TRAINING**

CONSULT YOUR NEAREST OFFICE OF THE **VETERANS ADMINISTRATION**

HELP FOR EUROPE

World War II left Europe in ruins. The United States was anxious that a poor, unstable Europe would be a breeding ground for political extremism, as happened after World War I (1914-1918). The United States gave Europe $17 billion in goods and aid to help rebuild its cities and economies. The official name of the program was the European Recovery Program (ERP). It was more usually referred to as the Marshall Plan for the Secretary of State, George Marshall, who devised and promoted it.

SOURCE EXPLORED

This government poster was aimed at veterans returning from the war. It shows men taking advantage of a new program that funded college education. Passed in 1944, the Serviceman's Readjustment Act—popularly known as the G.I. Bill of Rights—provided benefits through the Veterans Administration. Those benefits included low-cost mortgages (which helped to promote the move to the suburbs), college tuition and living expenses, and low-cost loans to set up businesses. By 1956, around 2.2 million veterans had used the bill to attend higher education. Another 5.6 million had trained for a new job. Altogether, the bill helped ease the return to civilian life, while also making sure the country had a skilled workforce to boost prosperity.

THE TRUMAN DOCTRINE

▶ President Harry S. Truman meets an admirer at a baseball game. Truman was president from 1945 to 1953.

With the Truman Doctrine of 1947, President Harry S. Truman reversed a century of U.S. foreign policy. In contrast to its former policy of isolationism, the United States was now willing to involve itself economically or militarily in conflicts wherever it saw a need. The doctrine was largely a response to the threat of Communism. It opened the way for U.S. involvement in wars all over the world.

On March 12, 1947, Truman explained to Congress why he wanted to help Greece defeat Communist rebels. The speech formed the basis of the Truman Doctrine.

" Nearly every nation must choose between alternative ways of life ... One way of life is based upon the will of the majority, and is distinguished by free institutions, representative government, free elections, guarantees of individual liberty, freedom of speech ... The second way of life is based upon the will of a minority forcibly imposed upon the majority. It relies upon terror and oppression ... and the suppression of personal freedoms. I believe that it must be the policy of the United States to support free peoples who are resisting attempted subjugation by armed minorities or by outside pressures. "

▲ Guards watch over captured Communist rebels during the emergency in Greece. The war lasted three years.

SOURCE EXPLORED

This photograph shows captured Greek Communists. In 1946 the Greek Communist Party, backed by the Soviet Union, rose up against the Greek government. A civil war that followed persuaded Truman to announce his doctrine in 1947. With British and then U.S. backing, the Greek government finally defeated the Communists in 1949.

THE KOREAN WAR

▲ U.S. troops display a captured North Korean flag during their campaign close to the Chinese border in North Korea.

The Truman Doctrine faced its first serious test in 1950, when Communist North Korea invaded South Korea. U.S. troops led the forces gathered by the United Nations to help South Korea. The U.S. government portrayed the war as a fight against Communism. North Korea was backed by the Soviet Union, and Chinese troops fought alongside the North Koreans. The war was unpopular in the United States. It lasted three years and ended with no outright winner. Both sides suffered heavy casualties.

◀ *Explosions mark an attack on enemy positions in the hills as U.S. soldiers make their way along a snowy road.*

SOURCE EXPLORED

This photograph shows U.S. soldiers watching explosions across a snowy landscape in North Korea. In the winter of 1950, temperatures fell to −32˚F (−35˚C). U.S. soldiers were ill-prepared. Their uniforms were inadequate, their guns jammed, their food froze, and many lost fingers or toes to frostbite.

By the middle of 1951, the fighting had become bogged down in trench warfare. Beverly Scott, an African-American platoon leader in the 14th Regiment, describes fighting in the hills just north of the North Korean border:

❝ We were eyeball to eyeball. Just 20 meters [65 feet] of no man's land between us. We couldn't move at all in the daytime without getting shot at. Machine-gun [fire] would come in, grenades, small-arms fire, all from within spitting distance. It was like World War I. We lived in a maze of bunkers and deep trenches. Some had been dug by previous occupants of the ridge. Some we dug ourselves. There were bodies strewn all over the place. Hundreds of bodies frozen in the snow. We could see the arms and legs sticking up. ❞

THE RED SCARE

Americans had long been wary about the threat of Communist agents, or "Reds," in the United States. There had been "red scares" in the 1920s and the 1930s. In 1950, a little-known senator from Wisconsin, Joseph McCarthy, claimed that 205 employees of the State Department were members of the Communist Party. He began a witch hunt seeking to expose Communists in the government, the media, and the U.S. military that lasted until 1954.

▼ *Actor Lionel Stander appears in front of the House Un-American Activities Committee investigating his links with Communism in 1953.*

McCarthy accused Americans from all walks of life of being Communist. The famous playwright Lillian Hellman describes appearing in front of the House Un-American Activities Committee:

" The room suddenly began to fill up behind me ... Representative Wood began to pound his gavel ... Was I a member of the Communist Party, had I been, what year had I stopped being? ... At times I couldn't follow the reasoning, at times I understood full well that in refusing to answer questions about membership in the Party I had, of course, trapped myself into a seeming admission that I once had been .... My hearing was over an hour and seven minutes after it began. "

SOURCE EXPLORED

Senator Joseph McCarthy (1908–1957) had an unremarkable career until 1950, when he claimed that many employees of the State Department were Communists. He was never able to prove his claim. In 1953, he began to investigate the U.S. Army. Eventually McCarthy's bullying of witnesses called before his committee led the Senate to condemn him in 1954. He died in disgrace in 1957.

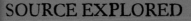

▲ McCarthy used his position on the Senate Committee on Government Operations to pursue people he thought were Communists.

THE ROSENBERG CASE

▶ Ethel and Julius Rosenberg leave court in a police van in 1951 after being found guilty of spying for the Soviet Union.

In 1951 Julius and Ethel Rosenberg, a married couple from New York, went on trial accused of passing atomic bomb secrets to the Russians. They were found guilty and sentenced to death. There was little evidence against them, and the sentence caused a storm of protest. The Rosenberg case, along with the convictions of the government official Alger Hiss and the British scientist Klaus Fuchs for spying, added weight to Joseph McCarthy's claims that the Communist threat was everywhere.

SOURCE EXPLORED

The *Los Angeles Times* of Saturday, June 20, 1953 announces the execution of the Rosenbergs. They had both died in the electric chair the previous evening. They were convicted of passing U.S. secrets to the Soviet Union. Julius Rosenberg had access to information about atomic bombs when he served as an electrical engineer in the U.S. Army Signal Corps. Critics of the convictions said they reflected U.S. paranoia about the possible nuclear threat from the Soviet Union. The Soviets had carried out nuclear tests in 1949, and many Americans feared they were close to building a usable bomb. In fact, later evidence suggested the Rosenbergs had indeed spied for the Soviets.

AS THEY SAW IT

" I consider your crime worse than murder ... I believe your conduct in putting into the hands of the Russians the A-Bomb ... has already caused the Communist aggression in Korea, with the resultant casualties ... and who knows but that millions more of innocent people may pay the price of your treason. "

—Judge Irving Kaufman sentences the Rosenbergs, April 5, 1951.

◄ *The Saturday edition of the* Los Angeles Times *announces the execution and notes that Eisenhower had rejected a plea for mercy.*

THE AGE OF THE AUTOMOBILE

By 1950, twice as many Americans owned cars than they had in 1935. The automobile transformed daily life. People could live in the suburbs and commute to work in the city. A dramatic improvement in roads and highways created a new kind of family vacation: the road trip. A whole infrastructure of motels, gas stations, and food outlets developed across the nation.

▼ *This car advertisement subtly links the automobile with the freedom of the open landscapes in the American West.*

▶ The Wigwam Motel in Holbrook, Arizona, was one of a local chain in which guests stayed in steel "tipis."

SOURCE EXPLORED

A 1950s automobile is on display at a restored motel. Before the fifties, there had been little call for motels as long-distance car journeys were comparatively rare. During the 1940s and the fuel shortages caused by World War II, the nation's highways had fallen into a poor state of repair. This was addressed at the start of the fifties. The federal government responded to the expansion of the suburbs and the boom in car ownership by building a 37,000-mile (59,500 km) Interstate Highway System. As families used the new roads to explore the country, they needed convenient places to break their journey. Motels (motor hotels) were like hotels except they offered a parking place as well as a room. Many motels also had swimming pools and restaurants on site to make the night stop even more convenient.

AS THEY SAW IT

" Left the cabins at 8 a.m. for another day of travel. Almost too beautiful to describe! Pigtail curves, beautiful bridges, tunnels through rock formations. A lot of hill climbing. At Lookout Point one would guess the ability to see 80 or 90 miles [130 or 145 km] away looking down onto beautiful valleys, etc. "

—Unknown writer, diary of a road trip to South Dakota, August 7, 1956

THE RISE OF THE SUBURBS

At the end of the 1940s, the United States faced a housing shortage. A federal program planned to construct five million new single-family houses on the edge of cities. Lying between the city and the countryside, the new suburbs came to define the 1950s. Cheap house prices, automobiles, and the expanded road system brought the suburbs within reach for many families.

▼ *This house advertisement showed buyers the standard plan of the homes being constructed in a new suburb.*

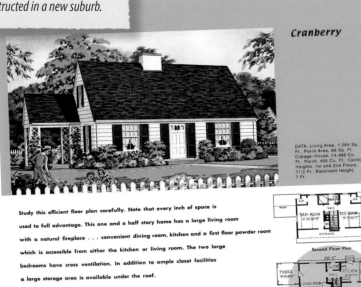

Cranberry

DATA: Living Area, 1,064 Sq. Ft.; Porch Area, 90 Sq. Ft.; Cubage-House, 14,480 Cu. Ft.; Porch, 495 Cu. Ft.; Ceiling Heights, 1st and 2nd Floors, 7 1/2 Ft.; Basement Height, 7 Ft.

Study this efficient floor plan carefully. Note that every inch of space is used to full advantage. This one and a half story home has a large living room with a natural fireplace . . . convenient dining room, kitchen and a first floor powder room which is accessible from either the kitchen or living room. The two large bedrooms have cross ventilation. In addition to ample closet facilities a large storage area is available under the roof.

A Kitchen and Utility Room Combined Is the Acme of Convenience

An Inviting Dining Space Encourages Work-saving Informality

▲ F. W. Woolworth Co. is among the stores lining the street in Levittown on Long Island, New York.

SOURCE EXPLORED

This photograph shows the shopping street in Levittown, Long Island, New York, in 1957. Levittown was the most famous of the fifties' housing developments. William Levitt introduced mass production to his family building firm. He anticipated huge demand for homes from former G.I.s and their young families, so he figured out a way to build standard timber houses on concrete bases cheaply and quickly. After the war, the Levitt firm bought 4,000 acres (1,620 hectares) of farmland on Long Island, and built the largest housing project in America. In just four years, Levitt built 17,447 houses on the Long Island site. At its peak, a house was completed every sixteen minutes. The houses all looked the same, but no one minded.

AS THEY SAW IT

" Bill Levitt didn't just build a community here—he built a world. We were young, all of us who moved to Levittown, and we thought Bill Levitt was the greatest man in the world. Imagine it—$10 deposit, $90 at settlement, and you had a house of your own! We had achieved the American Dream. "

WOMEN'S LIVES

Women's lives changed dramatically in the 1950s. During the war, millions of women went to work to replace the men who were away fighting. In the fifties, many women married and moved to the suburbs to raise a family. Being a homemaker became seen as a new kind of career. But many women still needed to earn money. Despite the idealized image of the full-time homemaker, by the end of the decade the number of women who worked outside the home had increased.

▶ *A woman does filing work in an office. During the fifties, women increasingly went out to work, often in clerical roles.*

▶ *This advertisement from a contemporary magazine shows a housewife in a kitchen full of modern appliances.*

SOURCE EXPLORED

The housewife in this advertisement calls a friend from her perfect kitchen while a meal cooks in the latest-style oven. Although the number of women in work rose, the fifties was also the decade of the stay-at-home mom.

As income levels rose, families could afford a middle-class lifestyle on one person's wage. The woman's job was to make sure the home ran smoothly: She shopped, cooked, cleaned, and drove the kids to their activities. In her spare time, she might meet other mothers—but housewives had little free time. Despite modern technology and new TV dinners, which meant that meals did not have to be prepared from scratch, women spent more time keeping house than their mothers and grandmothers. They were pressured by TV and magazine commercials like this one to keep their homes perfect.

LOST WOMEN

In 1957, writer Betty Friedan started to publish articles based on interviews about women's lives. Friedan noticed a growing dissatisfaction among college-educated women who were stay-at-home moms. They often felt bored and unfulfilled. Friedan dubbed this "the problem with no name." Her research later led to *The Feminine Mystique* (1963), a book that helped start the feminist movement.

GOLDEN AGE OF TV

If the 1940s was the age of the movies, the 1950s was the age of television. By the end of the decade, three-quarters of U.S. families had a TV set. Many owned color sets, which became more affordable after 1954. The number of television stations increased rapidly, paid for by advertisements. TV became the main source for popular culture, news, and commercial advertising.

▼ Dateline Disneyland *is among the highlights of Sunday night viewing in this listings magazine.*

SUNDAY   JULY 17

Cast

Socrates	Barry Jones
Aristophanes	E. G. Marshall
Crito	Shepperd Strudwick
Apollodorus	Richard Kiley
Plato	John Cassavetes

6:30 ⑩ The Christophers—Relig.

7:00 ② DEATH VALLEY DAYS
"Yaller." The story of the physical and mental struggles of Bruce Mathews to live up to his family's successful mining traditions. Ray Boyle as Bruce. (Film)

6 7 PEOPLE ARE FUNNY
Emcee Art Linkletter induces a male contestant to agree to wrestle with "the masked mauler." Unknown to the contestant, the "mauler" is big Buddy Baer.

9 56 REPORT FROM GENEVA
[SPECIAL] Howard K. Smith, chief European correspondent of CBS, narrates

7:30 ② 6 7 DATELINE DISNEYLAND

Walt Disney   Irene Dunne   Art Linkletter

Danny Thomas

[SPECIAL] Accompanied by California's Gov. Goodwin Knight, Walt Disney will arrive at Disneyland on the little Santa Fe and Disneyland railroad. Art Linkletter will also join Disney and act as co-emcee for the 90-minute extravaganza.

At Frontierland, Fess "Davy Crockett" Parker and Buddy Ebsen head the tour. Actress Irene Dunne will christen the paddle-wheel steamboat, "Mark Twain." Joining in the fun will be the "Make Room for Daddy" cast—Danny Thomas and his video family.

At Tomorrowland viewers visit the submarine Nautilus, used in Walt's film, "20,000 Leagues Under the Sea." There will be a tour of the world via the cyclorama, a trip to the moon via rocket, an autopia ride and a speed boat ride.

Fantasyland introduces many of the famous Disney cartoon characters, such as Mickey Mouse, the Three Little Pigs, Snow White and the Seven Dwarfs, Donald Duck, Pluto, Bambi, Cinderella, Alice in Wonderland. As the Pied Piper of 1955, Walt Disney leads hundreds of children across the drawbridge of the Sleeping Beauty castle, where they encounter mounted knights in shining armor, court jesters and acrobats.

Fess Parker

A-14   **TV GUIDE**

"The Summit: Report" A roundup of events that begins in Switzerland tomorrow. Eric Sevareid is commentator for a filmed report on Geneva. Changes in the American mood since the last time—1945—the Big Four met are suggested through films and sound track.

9 56 YOU ASKED FOR IT
1. Hawaiian surf riders. 2. A superstition about snakes is tested. 3. Sharpshooters with a blowgun. 4. The inside story of the Laguna Festival living paintings. 5. The auto daredevil stunt that killed nine men. Art Baker is the host. (Film)

7:30 ② 6 7 DATELINE DISNEY-LAND
[SPECIAL] This is a "live" 90-minute tour of the big new amusement park in Anaheim, Cal. Details on page A-14.

9 56 PRIVATE SECRETARY
Susie does her best to keep boss Peter Sands from forsaking the rush of the city for a quiet life down on the farm.

⑩ STUDIO 57—Drama
"Fish Widow." Sue and Joe are happily married, except for one thing. There's nothing fishy about the fact that hubby's been hooked by rod-and-reel fever.

Cast

Sue	Pat Carroll
Joe	Joe Allen, Jr.
Ted	Ward Wood
Mike	Jim Hayward
Art	Jan Arvan

⑯ THE BIG PICTURE

8:00 9 ⑩ ⑯ TOAST OF TOWN
It's musical-comedy star Ethel Merman who's subbing for vacationing Ed Sullivan tonight. She'll sing a selection of the songs for which she's best known and join in a duet with Russell Nype, who starred with her in the stage version of "Call Me Madam." Also on the guest list are: operatic singer Gloria Lane, who starred on Broadway in Gian-Carlo Menotti's "The Saint of Bleecker Street"; "Prof. Backwards," Jimmy Edmondson; the Peiro Brothers, jugglers; and the Rhythmettes, a precision-dance group. Meet Ed Sullivan, gentleman farmer, in next week's TV GUIDE.

9:00 ② STAR AND THE STORY
"They." An elderly inmate of a sanitarium decides to revolt against the "Theys" in the world. Thomas Mitchell. (Film)

6 7 TV PLAYHOUSE
"Man on Spikes," adapted by Eliot Asinof from his novel of the same name. The baseball saga tells of an excellent player who is kept in the minor leagues by his team. His wife objects to the tedium of years of makeshift living in small towns, but he goes on, hoping that his big break will finally come. Asinof's brother-in-law, Marlon Brando, has purchased the film rights to "Man on Spikes."

Cast

Mike Kutner	Warren Stevens
Ellen Kutner	Janet Ward
Al Tracy	Ned Glass
Herb Mattison	Bill Zuckert
Jim	Frank Campanella
Max	James Millhollin
Pete	Robert Morse
Larrabie	Terry Carter
Sam	Jeff Harris

9 ⑩ ⑯ 56 G. E. THEATER
Joan Crawford stars in "The Road to Edinburgh." An American newspaperwoman is driving to Edinburgh in order to cover a story. Her car breaks down and a man offers her some help. In return she gives him a lift but soon begins to regret her offer. (Film)

Cast

Mary Andrews	Joan Crawford
Man	John Sutton
Boy	Christopher Cook
Soldier	Chuck Connors
Policeman	Jack Raine

9:30 ② GROUCHO MARX—Quiz

② STAGE 7—Drama
"Emergency." A message from an old friend contemplating suicide, sends a man on a desperate race against time and across continents. (Film)

Cast

Alan	Lee Bowman
Mary	Jean Byron
Billy	Christopher Dark
Elle	Angela Greene
Beth Leyton	Frances Mercer

TV GUIDE   A-15

SUNDAY

SOURCE EXPLORED

The holiday issue of *Look* magazine from 1956 features the cast of *I Love Lucy*, the most popular situation comedy, or sitcom, of the decade. Lucille Ball played Lucy Ricardo, the starstruck wife of Cuban bandleader Ricky Ricardo (Desi Arnaz, Ball's real-life husband). The show ran on CBS from 1951 until 1957, and was the first show to have ten million viewers for a single episode. It was so popular that Marshall Fields, the Chicago department store, changed its weekly clearance sale to avoid clashing with it. In real life, Lucille Ball was a smart businesswoman and a pioneer TV producer. She was not at all like her character.

▲ *Lucille Ball and husband Desi Arnaz appear with their on-screen son on the cover of* Look *in 1956.*

ED MURROW

The journalist Ed Murrow became popular for his radio broadcasts from London during World War II. After the war, he became the trusted face of current affairs on television. He fronted *See It Now*, a news show. On March 9, 1954, Murrow broadcast an edition about Senator Joseph McCarthy's witch hunts. It exposed the senator's bullying tactics and sensationalist speeches. The show marked the beginning of the end of McCarthy's witch hunts.

FREE TIME

Americans with free time and money had many ways to relax in the fifties. They could watch TV, go to the movies, and take road trips. Fads took the country by storm, such as the Hula-hoop in 1957. In the suburbs, a craze for the card game canasta was later displaced by the board game Scrabble. Many people took up new hobbies. "Do it yourself," or DIY, became popular, particularly with men. Women's magazines reported the latest trends and provided tips on how to upgrade the family home.

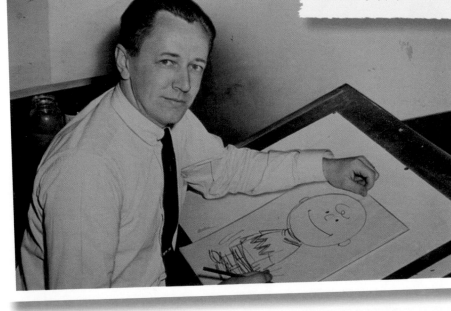

▼ Charles Schulz poses with a drawing of his creation, Charlie Brown. The ups and downs of Charlie's life were hugely popular with readers.

◀ *This replica of Ray Kroc's first McDonald's restaurant stands on the site of the original in Des Plaines, Illinois.*

SOURCE EXPLORED

In 1955, two distinctive golden arches appeared above a McDonald's fast food restaurant west of Chicago. This photograph shows a re-creation of founder Ray Kroc's first restaurant. By 1959, there were 145 McDonald's across the country. The rise in popularity of fast-food restaurants coincided with the boom in driving. On the road, people wanted to eat without the delay of full-service dining. From the start, McDonald's faced competition. The first Sonic had opened as Top Hat Drive-In in 1953 and Burger King as Insta-Burger King in the same year. Colonel Sanders's Kentucky Fried Chicken appeared in 1955. The fast-food revolution also affected how people ate at home. Sales of fries, ketchup, and pickles rose dramatically.

NEW COMIC STRIP

On October 2, 1950, a new comic strip appeared in many newspapers. It featured a large-headed boy named Charlie Brown and his dog, Snoopy. The cartoon was entitled *Peanuts*, created by Charles M. Schulz. Schulz drew the adventures of Charlie Brown and his friends daily, with a special Sunday strip, until December 1999: a total of nearly 17,900 episodes. The strip was syndicated in more than 2,600 newspapers, and readers across the country followed the adventures of Charlie Brown. The stories of his perpetual failures made him one of the best-loved cartoon characters of all time.

AT THE MOVIES

In the early 1950s, Hollywood was in a slump. People were staying home to watch TV. To win back audiences, moviemakers tried new ideas. Alongside musicals and westerns, Hollywood produced blockbusters with huge budgets. Studios also revived the kind of screwball comedies that were popular in the thirties, with glamorous stars such as Marilyn Monroe. They also investigated the troubles of young people in U.S. society.

▼ *Marilyn Monroe starred in some of the most successful film comedies of the fifties, such as Some Like it Hot (1959).*

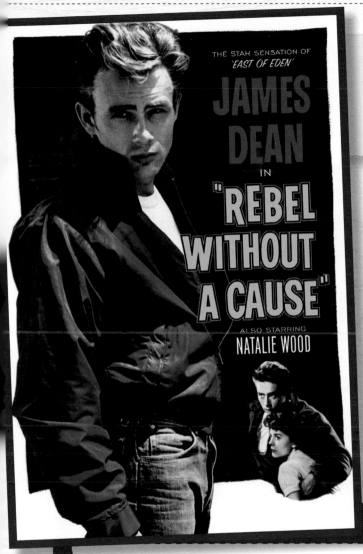

THE STAR SENSATION OF
'EAST OF EDEN'

JAMES
DEAN

IN

"REBEL
WITHOUT
A CAUSE"

ALSO STARRING
NATALIE WOOD

◀ *In* Rebel Without a Cause, *James Dean played a troubled teenager who arrives at a new school and gets into trouble for breaking the rules.*

SOURCE EXPLORED

In 1955, a movie appeared with a lead actor who would define the feelings of a generation. In only his second film, *Rebel Without a Cause*, James Dean starred as a teenage loner rebelling against the rules of society. By the time the movie was released in the fall of 1955, Dean was dead. He died in a high-speed automobile accident on a California highway. His first major movie, *East of Eden* (1955), had made him a star, but it was *Rebel Without a Cause* that made him a teenage idol. Young men saw him as a symbol of their own sense of rebellion, while young women were attracted to his good looks and sensitivity. A year after Dean's death, the Warner Brothers Studio was receiving seven thousand letters a month from grief-stricken fans.

SPORTS HEROES

▲ Althea Gibson coaches a group of teenagers. Gibson became the first nonwhite player to win a tennis Grand Slam title when she won the French Open in 1956.

In the 1950s, sports led the way in racial desegregation, with pioneers such as Jackie Robinson in baseball and Althea Gibson in tennis. Baseball was the most popular spectator sport, but both football and basketball were gaining fans. Football grew more popular in 1950, when unlimited substitutions were introduced. In basketball, the Minneapolis Lakers dominated.

SOURCE EXPLORED

Jackie Robinson wears a Brooklyn Dodgers cap on the cover of this comic book from 1951. African Americans had played in their own league until 1947. Robinson broke the color barrier of Major League Baseball when he was hired to play for the Dodgers. Robinson, who earned three Most Valuable Player awards, paved the way for other African Americans. They included future Hall-of-Famers Larry Doby (Cleveland Indians, 1947–1959), Roy Campanella (Brooklyn Dodgers, 1948–1958), and Willie Mays, whose career began with the New York Giants in 1951 and ended with the Mets in 1973. Integration brought the abolition of the so-called Negro Leagues, which had first been held in the 1880s.

A Fawcett Publication

Jackie Robinson

NO. 5

10¢

Special!
INSIDE THE
DODGER TRAINING
CAMP!
READ
**ROOKIE
ON TRIAL!**

18

▲ The cover of this 1951 comic book features a portrait of Jackie Robinson and an inset of him fielding at second base.

AS THEY SAW IT

" After the game, Jackie Robinson came into our clubhouse and shook my hand ... Here was a player who had without doubt suffered more abuse and more taunts and more hatred than any player in the history of the game. And he had made a special effort to compliment and encourage a young white kid from Oklahoma. "

–Mickey Mantle, New York Yankees, after defeating the Brooklyn Dodgers in the World Series, 1952

THE RISE OF THE TEENAGER

▲ *Teenage girls take a dancing lesson. The classroom walls are covered with photographs of movie stars and singers.*

In the fifties, teenagers came to be seen as a distinct social group. Previously, people in their teens had simply been young adults. By the mid-1950s, there were 16.5 million U.S. teenagers. They stayed at school longer than their parents had done and many of them went on to college. With work postponed until their twenties and with many part-time jobs available, these were the first young adults to have their own money and the free time to enjoy it. A whole world of fashion, cars, movies, and music emerged to satisfy the new teenage market.

The new music teenagers listened to was called rock 'n' roll. Michael Ventura, journalist and cultural critic, remembers the impact the music had:

" There's no way to grasp the subversive force of this now-innocent-sounding music unless you can feel a little of what it meant to be a kid hearing it as it was played for the first time. It was music that was made for teenagers and scared the hell out of adults; it was taboo-shattering music about—gasp—sex and racial commingling. That's why records were burned, censorship laws were passed, and some lives were ruined. Because this was the Devil's music, and it was threatening the status quo. But you couldn't stop anything this real. It belonged to the kids and only the kids. It set them apart. It was their freedom. It is still so today. "

SOURCE EXPLORED

The jukebox provided the soundtrack for teenage life. Invented in the 1890s, the jukebox contained records of the latest hits. Using a combination of letters and numbers, the listener chose a song from the index and the machine selected and played the song. With its chrome grills and bright colors, the jukebox was often seen in drugstores, bars, coffee shops, and diners of the fifties.

◀ *Teenagers select a song on a Wurlitzer jukebox in a coffee bar.*

ROCK 'N' ROLL

Blending rhythm and blues (R&B) and country music, rock 'n' roll was a long way from the smooth ballads of the early 1950s. In 1955, Bill Haley and the Comets had the first rock 'n' roll hit with "Rock Around the Clock." The song featured in the movie *Blackboard Jungle* and caused a sensation. Other rock 'n' roll stars included the African Americans Chuck Berry and Little Richard and the white performers Jerry Lee Lewis and Buddy Holly. The singer who really changed the face of music was a young trucker from Memphis, Tennessee. His name was Elvis Aaron Presley.

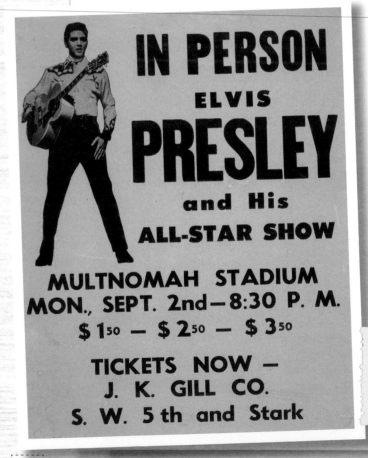

IN PERSON
ELVIS
PRESLEY
and His
ALL-STAR SHOW

MULTNOMAH STADIUM
MON., SEPT. 2nd—8:30 P. M.
$ 1⁵⁰ — $ 2⁵⁰ — $ 3⁵⁰

TICKETS NOW —
J. K. GILL CO.
S. W. 5th and Stark

◀ *This poster promotes an Elvis Presley show in Portland, Oregon, in September 1957. By then, Elvis was the biggest star in the country.*

SOURCE EXPLORED

Excited girls autograph a poster for the Elvis Presley movie *Love Me Tender*, which premiered in 1956. By then, Presley was a superstar, with hits such as "Heartbreak Hotel" and "Hound Dog" and an eager teenage following. Just three years earlier, in 1953, Presley had paid $4 to record a song for his mother at Sun Records in Memphis. When Sun's owner Sam Phillips heard Presley's voice, he knew he had discovered a star. For young Americans, Presley's performance was as important as his voice. Elvis "the Pelvis" swivelled his hips in a way many older adults found offensive. His appearance on the *Ed Sullivan Show* in September 1956 drew the largest TV audience there had been to date, with sixty million viewers.

▲ Teenage Elvis fans autograph a poster for his movie *Love Me Tender* (1956).

AS THEY SAW IT

"Without preamble, the three-piece band cuts loose. In the spotlight, the lanky singer flails furious rhythms on his guitar, every now and then breaking a string. In a pivoting stance, his hips swing sensuously from side to side and his entire body takes on a frantic quiver, as if he had swallowed a jackhammer. "

—*Time* magazine describes an Elvis Presley live concert, May 15, 1956

AFRICAN AMERICANS

During the fifties, much of U.S. society remained racially segregated. In many places, white and black Americans could not share things, from washrooms and buses to schools and housing. New suburbs such as those built by William Levitt were not open to African-American families. During the decade, however, laws such as the **Civil Rights Act of 1957** slowly started to end racial divisions.

▼ *African-American and white schoolgirls wait in line in the integrated Barnard School in Washington, D.C. in May 1955.*

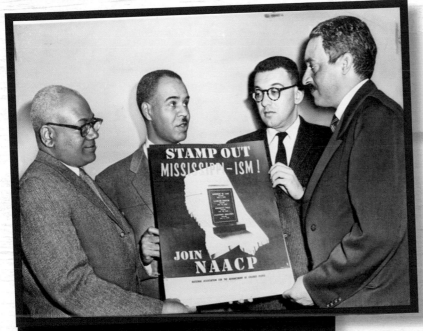

◀ *The leaders of the NAACP display a poster aimed at recruiting more members to support its civil rights campaign.*

SOURCE EXPLORED

This 1956 photograph shows leaders of the National Association for the Advancement of Colored People (NAACP) with a poster calling for the end of "Mississippi-ism," or racial bias in the state. They are (from left to right) Henry L. Moon, Roy Wilkins, Herbert Hill, and Thurgood Marshall. Founded in 1909, the NAACP led the fight to end segregation and ensure equality for African Americans. It led the fight in the courts that ended segregation in schools with the 1954 Supreme Court decision, *Brown v. Board of Education*. It also led the bus boycott in Montgomery, Alabama in 1955, which lasted 381 days and brought integration on the city's public transportation network. The NAACP laid the foundations for the Civil Rights Movement of the 1960s.

BLACK MONDAY

Thomas Pickens Brady, a judge in Mississippi and a member of the White Citizens' Council, published a pamphlet named *Black Monday* after Monday, May 17, 1954. That was the day the Supreme Court handed down its decision in *Brown v. Board of Education*, which ended segregation in the nation's schools. Brady called for the abolition of the NAACP and the creation of a 49th state—there were then only 48—where African Americans would be forced to live separately from white people.

EISENHOWER AND FOREIGN AFFAIRS

Dwight D. Eisenhower won the 1952 presidential election by a huge number of votes. "I Like Ike" Eisenhower was a general who led the D-Day invasion in World War II. He was president for the rest of the fifties. For advice on foreign affairs, Eisenhower relied on his secretary of state, John Foster Dulles. Dulles believed the United States should not just contain Communism but should also win back territory seized by Communists. The policy shaped foreign affairs throughout the fifties.

◄ Eisenhower had little political experience but was popular largely because of his successful war record.

◀ *The presidential motorcade makes its way into the Afghan capital, Kabul, on December 9, 1959. Eisenhower was the first U.S. president to visit the country.*

SOURCE EXPLORED

On December 9, 1959, President Eisenhower drives into Kabul, Afghanistan. Thousands of Afghans braved the low temperatures to catch a glimpse of Eisenhower as he was driven into Kabul from Bagram Airfield. Eisenhower was on an official visit to meet King Zahir Shah as part of a U.S. goodwill trip to Central Asia and the Middle East. He knew that Afghanistan was important in preventing the spread of Communism and that the Soviet Union had been pouring aid into the country since 1955. To counter the Communist threat from Russia, Eisenhower offered U.S. aid to the Afghan government.

DOMINO THEORY

Throughout the fifties, the United States became increasingly involved in the countries of Southeast Asia: Vietnam, Laos, and Cambodia. It first supported the French colonial rulers and later supplied military aid and personnel in an effort to contain Communism. Eisenhower defended U.S. involvement in the region on the grounds that if one country fell to Communism they all would—like dominoes in a row. This so-called Domino Theory shaped the U.S. foreign policy that resulted in the Vietnam War.

THE SPACE RACE BEGINS

▲ Russians walk past a model of the Sputnik III *satellite at an exhibition held in Moscow in August 1959 .*

U.S. leaders believed the best way to keep the peace was to show the Soviet Union that it would lose any nuclear war. Known as deterrence, the strategy led both sides to improve their nuclear weapons. As a spin-off, they competed to develop space technology. Most Americans assumed that U.S. technology was far ahead of that of the Soviets. That changed when the Soviets launched *Sputnik I*, the first artifical satellite, into space in October 1957.

SOURCE EXPLORED

These seven astronauts were part of Project Mercury, the first U.S. human spaceflight program. Project Mercury was launched in 1959 by the new National Aeronautics and Space Administration (NASA). NASA was created largely in response to the Soviet launch of *Sputnik I* in October 1957. The launch had stunned most Americans, who believed the United States was winning the space war. Now NASA wanted to put the first man into space. On May 5, 1961, Alan Shepard became the first American in space when he completed a suborbital flight—but the Soviet Union had already sent Yuri Gagarin into space one month earlier.

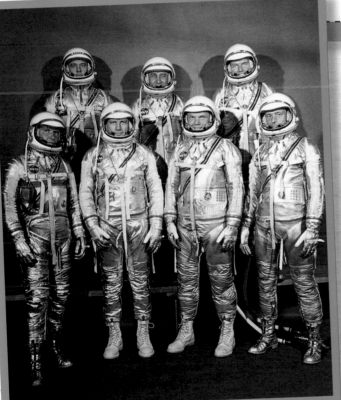

▲ *The Mercury Seven pose in their spacesuits. Most were experienced test pilots from the U.S. Air Force.*

AS THEY SAW IT

❝ At a sudden signal, we would drop from our chairs ... and crouch and wait until the A-bomb had fallen .... What made this so unreal, even to nine- and ten-year-olds, was what would happen if an atomic bomb fell on New York City. Concentric circles displayed the consequences: if the bomb exploded at the Empire State Building, everything up to 110th Steet would be vaporized. ❞

—Jeff Greenfield recalls nuclear bomb drills at school in the 1950s

REVOLUTION IN CUBA

During the nineteenth century and the first half of the twentieth century, the island of Cuba had been a favorite destination for America's rich, who flocked to its clubs, casinos, and beaches. The Cuban dictator, Fulgencio Batista, allowed the rich to live well at the expense of the poor. In July 1953, a campaign to get rid of Batista was launched by Fidel Castro and his supporter, "Che" Guevara. The campaign was a failure but the revolution succeeded on January 1, 1959.

◀ The Argentine revolutionary Che Guevara—seen here in a mural in Havana, Cuba—helped lead the overthrow of the Batista regime.

SOURCE EXPLORED

The leader of the Cuban Revolution, Fidel Castro, arrives in Washington, D.C., on April 15, 1959, four months after overthrowing Fulgencio Batista. Castro was invited by the American Society of Newspaper Editors. President Eisenhower refused to meet Castro. He and his government believed Castro was a Communist, as they thought was shown when he seized U.S.-owned property in Cuba. In fact, Castro was not originally a Communist. He had hoped to receive aid from the United States for Cuba. When no U.S. help was forthcoming, however, he turned to the Soviet Union. The Soviets were more than happy to oblige.

▲ *Fidel Castro arrives in the United States in April 1959. His hopes of receiving U.S. aid for Cuba were to be disappointed.*

GUATEMALA

In 1954, the Central Intelligence Agency (CIA) overthrew the elected president of Guatemala, Jacobo Arbenz, in a secret raid. Arbenz's election had followed the overthrow of the U.S.-backed military dictator, Jorge Ubico. The U.S. government feared the country would become Communist. If it did, John Foster Dulles argued, the rest of Central America might follow. The invasion was seen as being vital to prevent the possible spread of Communism through Mexico to the United States itself.

THE START OF THE SIXTIES

Despite the peace and economic prosperity of America in the fifties, many Americans rejected the values of the majority of the nation. Those who were unhappy included bored housewives, suppressed African Americans, dissatisfied teenagers, and Beat poets who expressed their alienation in words. The mood would continue to build into the sixties.

▼ *In 1957, Jack Kerouac published* On the Road, *a book that summed up the so-called Beat movement of writers who were against authority.*

◀ *Since the first edition of the book appeared in 1951,* The Catcher in the Rye *has sold sixty-five million copies.*

DELINQUENTS

In 1956, William Clement Kvaraceus published *Forecasting Juvenile Delinquency.* The book noted that half of all robberies in U.S. cities were carried out by people under the age of twenty-one. It described this as "juvenile delinquency." No one could agree on what had caused the worrying trend. Some argued it was because parents were too busy to look after their children. Others blamed the rising number of divorces.

SOURCE EXPLORED

One book in the 1950s captured the feelings of the youth of the time and became an emblem for that generation: J. D. Salinger's *The Catcher in the Rye*, published in 1951. It was written for adults but soon became popular among teenagers. Its themes of teenage concerns and alienation spoke to a generation. Salinger's main character and narrator, Holden Caulfield, is in the hospital in California. From his bed, he describes a week in New York City during Christmas break after he has been expelled from his exclusive private school. Salinger often uses vulgar language to tell a story of cynicism and of a world that adults simply do not understand.

TIMELINE

1947	**March 12:** President Truman announces the Truman Doctrine to Congress; it enables the United States to send aid to Greece and Turkey to fight the spread of Communism.
	April 15: Jackie Robinson breaks the color bar in Major League Baseball when he debuts for the Brooklyn Dodgers.
	June 5: George C. Marshall proposes the provision of aid to help Europe recover after the war. It was known as the Marshall Plan.
1948	**April 1:** The Soviet Union blockades the Allied areas of West Berlin; the blockade lasts until September 1949.
	December: State Department official Alger Hiss is indicted for passing atomic intelligence to the Soviet Union.
1950	**June 25:** North Korean troops, armed with Soviet weapons, invade South Korea, beginning the Korean War. U.S. forces are authorized to join the conflict five days later.
	October 2: The first Peanuts cartoon strip is published.
	November 26: Chinese troops join North Korea in a campaign to push UN forces back south toward the 38th Parallel.
1951	**March 29:** Ethel and Julius Rosenberg are found guilty of espionage; they are executed on June 19, 1953.
	June 15: The first episode of TV comedy I Love Lucy is broadcast.
	July 16: J.D. Salinger's book The Catcher in the Rye is published.
1952	**November 4:** Former Allied general Dwight D. Eisenhower wins the presidential election for the Republican Party.
1953	**July 27:** A peace treaty is signed, bringing an end to the fighting in Korea.
	August 19: The CIA helps plan a coup to overthrow the government in Iran.
	October 30: President Eisenhower authorizes the expansion of the U.S. nuclear arsenal.
	December 30: The first color television sets go on sale in America.
1954	**February 23:** The first large-scale program of vaccination against polio begins.

April 22: *Senator Joseph McCarthy begins televised hearings into Communist sympathizers in the U.S. Army.*

May 17: *The U.S. Supreme Court rules racial segregation of schools unconstitutional in* Brown v. Board of Education.

December 2: *The Senate votes to condemn Senator Joseph McCarthy for his behavior during the Army hearings.*

1955

February 12: *The United States agrees to train South Vietnamese troops to help fight Communist guerrillas.*

April 15: *Ray Kroc opens his first McDonald's franchise in Des Plaines, Illinois, after an agreement the previous year with the McDonald brothers who founded the chain.*

July 17: *Walt Disney opens Disneyland in Anaheim, California.*

September 30: *Movie star James Dean dies in a car crash in California.*

December 1: *Seamstress Rosa Parks refuses to give up her seat on a bus to a white passenger in Montgomery, Alabama, sparking an African-American boycott of transportation in the city.*

1956

January 27: *Elvis Presley releases "Heartbreak Hotel," his first number-one single and a million-seller.*

June 29: *The Federal Aid Highway Act is signed, creating the interstate highway system.*

November 6: *Eisenhower is easily elected to a second term as president.*

1957

April 29: *The U.S. Congress approves a civil rights bill.*

October 4: *The Soviet Union launches the first space satellite, Sputnik.*

1958

January 31: *The Army launches the first U.S. space satellite, Explorer 1.*

1959

January 7: *The United States recognizes the new government of Cuba, led by Fidel Castro, after the revolution.*

April 9: *NASA selects the first seven astronauts for the Mercury Project.*

GLOSSARY

alienation A sense of not belonging.

atomic Relating to an atom or other small chemical particle.

Beat A writer or artist belonging to a movement that rejected conventional mid-century values.

boycott To cease buying goods or services from a particular supplier as a protest.

bunker A reinforced underground shelter.

color bar A rule that prevents black people doing something.

Communism A political system based on a lack of private ownership.

conformity Complying with the general rules and attitudes of society.

delinquency Minor crimes, usually committed by young people.

democracy A political system based on elected governments and private property.

desegregation The elimination of differences in the treatment of different races.

deterrence A strategy based on preventing an enemy from acting by threatening a destructive response.

dictator A ruler who has absolute power.

infrastructure The basic physical structures needed by a society, such as roads, bridges, and power lines.

integrated Having no difference in the treatment of different races.

isolationism A policy of avoiding involvement in the political affairs of other countries.

mortgage A loan made in order to buy property, such as a house.

optimism A feeling of hopefulness about the future.

prosperity The state of having a thriving economy.

segregated Separated from others, particularly on the basis of race.

subjugation The removal of rights from a group of people.

suburbs A residential district on the edge of a city.

subversive Acting to damage or destroy an established system.

syndicated Published at the same time in a number of newspapers.

witch hunt A campaign against someone with views that are seen as a threat to society.

FURTHER INFORMATION

Books

Corrigan, Jim. *The 1950s: The American Decade*. Amazing Decades in Photos. Berkeley Heights, NJ: Enslow Publishers Ltd, 2010.

George, Enzo. *The Korean War: Showdown with China*. Voices of War. New York: Cavendish Square Publishing, 2014.

Hansen, Sarah. *Dwight D. Eisenhower* Presidents of the USA. Mankato, MN: The Child's World, Inc, 2008.

Krieg, Katherine. *The Postwar Era: 1945–Early 1970s*. The Story of the United States. Minneapolis, MN: ABDO Publishing Company, 2014.

Lindop, Edmund, and Sarah De Capua. *America in the 1950s*. Decades of Twentieth-Century America. Minneapolis, MN: Twenty-First Century Books, 2009.

McNeese, Tim. *The Cold War and Postwar America: 1946–1963*. Discovering U.S. History. New York: Chelsea House Publishers, 2010.

Schwartz, Richard Alan. *The 1950s*. Eyewitness History. New York: Facts on File, Inc, 2003.

Websites

www.history.com/topics/korean-war
History.com pages about the Korean War, with videos.

www.history.com/topics/1950s
History.com analysis of the decade, with videos and numerous links.

www.shmoop.com/1950s/society.html
Overview of the 1950s for students on Shmoop.com.

ushistory1950.weebly.com/index.html
A site about U.S. society in the 1950s, with numerous thematic essays.

Publisher's note to educators and parents: Our editors have carefully reviewed these websites to ensure that they are suitable for students. Many websites change frequently, however, and we cannot guarantee that a site's future contents will continue to meet our high standards of quality and educational value. Be advised that students should be closely supervised whenever they access the Internet.

INDEX